REVERIES OF A SOLITARY BIKER

ALSO BY CATRIONA STRANG

Busted (with Nancy Shaw)
*Corked**
The Gorge: Selected Writing of Nancy Shaw (ed.)*
Light, Sweet, Crude (with Nancy Shaw)
Low Fancy

* Published by Talonbooks

REVERIES

of a solitary biker

[poems]

CATRIONA STRANG

TALONBOOKS

Talonbooks
278 East First Avenue, Vancouver, British Columbia, Canada v5T 1A6
www.talonbooks.com

First printing: 2017

Typeset in Jenson
Printed and bound in Canada on 100% post-consumer recycled paper

Interior and cover design by Typesmith
Cover illustration by Kelly Haydon

Talonbooks gratefully acknowledges the financial support of the Canada Council for the Arts, the Government of Canada through the Canada Book Fund, and the Province of British Columbia through the British Columbia Arts Council and the Book Publishing Tax Credit.

LIBRARY AND ARCHIVES CANADA CATALOGUING IN PUBLICATION

Strang, Catriona, author
    Reveries of a solitary biker : poems / Catriona Strang.

Includes bibliographical references.
ISBN 978-1-77201-180-7 (SOFTCOVER)

    I. TITLE.

PS8587.T679R48 2017   C811'.54   C2017-905038-9

for the frail fucken flowers

because we don't get to be *flâneurs*

—DOROTHY TRUJILLO LUSK

CONTENTS

DIAMONDS [1]

CLUBS [17]

HEARTS [33]

SPADES [49]

EPILOGUE [65]
ON NOT LOOKING INTO CHAPMAN'S HOMER

AFTERWORD [74]

ACKNOWLEDGMENTS [77]

DIAMONDS

A

March 14, 2014

"imagine us"

in the absence
of her voices
exactly how much
entrancing exactitude
can be expected

2

March 4, 2014

two great
hostiles I can't
help: naked, shameless,
direct, brutal
suckered

we find new wants
and our shorts
are timed

3

January 21, 2014

discord, disruption, and
despair, what a
strange delusion

discussion could be
a vessel
or derisive vessel
visibly risable

at nearly every turn
such murky marvels

4

September 10, 2013

damage taken up
the ultimate act of
joyous unexpected

comes from their now (the
joy of her, the
spangled head)

so that activities are social forces
like a woman using
a staircase

5

January 24, 2014: the cracked kettle

we have been mercied
our troubles converted

we feel no liking
who might
scuff at anyone

6

January 6, 2014

come closer kindling
a kinder closure

righteously complicated
composure

same scaffolding
different times

I'm rarely
on the job
rarely kitted

kinder
don't
come
close

7

February 26, 2014

how variegated discrepancies
implode, rather than
dispose (*"we cannot dispense
with palliative measures"*)

intoxicating satisfaction
more than a consolation

8

at least we have voiced our displeasure

9

dare I say ought
I dare say we might

thinking of a strategic
cycle, I've not been
a subject as much as
anyway, anymore

striving
to underachieve

10

October 8, 2013

to admit
interest primarily
our labour acknowledged
we insist

it's no man's world
virtue in the smell
of grass, water seeks
or seeps low

"desired I never none"
Of course it's
not allowed

J

It was a beautiful mishap. Who could have imagined that I would be anything but receptive? From now on, we will express value in numbers of floors swept. As the foregoing analysis should already have demonstrated, I have long been mystified by the multitude of signs advertising "self storage": I dare you to bike my ride. Nor is this all; having yet to rust, we bid farewell to the deadly ideologue, as once we bid farewell to our taste for subsumption. It's a dark matter, and I reserve the right to chain my mind. Yet again, we are all collateral damage.

Q

January 14, 2014

"no transcendence, no deliverance, no novel"

of another ilk all
together, a partial
extinction, a cultural
bell

I might, if I could
manage to bilk myself

(*astride which
anxious gear?*)

of course there lurks
our own ill-
hulked constitution

April 2, 2014

might we collide
or do I collude?

CLUBS

A

November 11, 2013

"nothing can give us security"

a breach once
made, extrapolate
with certainty

must we all be improved
by industry's justice, by affable
charity, by Monday mornings
       (for are we not *FANATICS*)

sufficient
      to blast
           her character

2

September 2, 2013

I've frankly never
geared more
incredible permutations of

here I have found
(do we all have
our bodies?)

oh tentative shift
what sort of
hope is
this

we, not I,
have not found?

also we
must discuss
land   use

3

we need
not marvel
at knot-
weed

4

extremely intricate

conditions will

degenerate extremely

5

scarcely two wheeling years
sheers whole legions
cheering (*inside which
room?*) for the overhead
projector; no invites no
fracking, but if freed
I'll assume adjacent
hustles; as I bellow
my manifesto, I stagger
over negotiating cables

6

avert or avoid, articles
may have
shifted, and
there's still no sacrifice
for substitution
but come on
and bilk my
ride, I'm dressed
in leaves, I chafe
at my constraints, I've been
much stuck

7

September 16, 2013

nor much possibility, either
like truly proscribed and
identifiable
to stave
off

unclear on

nor do I understand
that a moral tablet
does not consist

regular practices involved

8

but more in the way of
how did this phrase turn
"innovative"? my point has
been automated, kindled
double clients balk
and now allow small
notes, a micro-targeted
realism, which we hail
as a has-been, a retro-
refutation, a saddled
subject

9

Who is to say who we are? Despite the brandishment of intricate harmonies, my head has been tuned to the pitch of a strange instrument, and all the difficulties which perplex us are beyond rectification, if I do not deceive myself – but what am I saying here? I ought to proceed with order & method, but such an undertaking is beyond me. I am bewildered by those who behave as though, having drunk from the modern cup, they now can and must sell all, and simple pleasures must vanish. Perhaps it would be best here to avert your gaze; like the snail with its shell, I appall myself.

10

"do you want Chinese, or chicken and beer?"

J

♣

at least our displeasure has been made apparent

Q

I can perceive neither profits nor remedies. What remains is a fragile chapter, composed of trauma, addiction, and consumption, but only in a sardonic sense. Despite the soft soul of compassion, who among us has not been compelled by necessity? But that is already in our distant past; the reveries of my stormy youth have long since been sold. What a host of intricate, fragile problems fills the modern cup; perhaps all its resolutions are mere folly, but they cruise decisive significance. Ours is at most a delegated originality.

K

at least our displeasure has been made known

HEARTS

A

November 20, 2013: of overkill

"what a long time it requires to know ourselves"

will sup all
(a great pleasure)
introducing no less
sop than the pleasure it
diffused: a sensibility
wounded

(*a fine example*
of overkill) note before
and early:
although astride
she might
be right

2

February 4, 2014

"shrewdly relapsing into repose"

sounds like
co-option, sounds like miss
representation, sounds
like handbooks
for everyone

multiplication sounds
like a mountainous
abstraction, sounds
like cascading
monstrous monstrous

3

October 21, 2013

because the world is such

our tempestuous fragility
a mobbish jolt
(see how we're moving along)
a sustained interest in
constriction

at least it's a structured hell

4

September 20, 2013

giving voice to
all this grief

I know that I am
nerving up
my work

5

January 28, 2014

"joking with clenched teeth"

reproach me
cornered

or maybe it was
yesterday we had
an agreeable walk

6

November 26, 2013

some tactically
astute revelation
a social
fact, oh rigid
imperfect fervour

I'm nearly
unconvinced, little
specifics genuinely
forgotten, *talk*
about a rat
trap scrutiny

only by
appeals to
body parts

7

how can
we liken
our most entwined
entanglements
(every moss, every
lichen) so mulch-loose
linked; your looping's
merely loped

8

a document of possibilities

And here it becomes apparent that common intentions are as apples dropped by habit, and by patient accumulation also. Even a wild parent will at times determine how far new wants shall be entertained. I will here only allude to the successive variations bursting forth from the tree of industry; such facts are of plain signification. I am thoroughly convinced, and yet by some monstrosity still I presume to doubt. We have witnessed considerable deviation, but so many causes tend to obscure this result. In the spectre of great hostile camps, ensconced on stolen land, we continue to replace old wants. Whose habits must at all times be accounted for? How entirely vague are the considerable deviations we find through the opening of that wide door labelled "Conjecture." Not for the first time, I was much struck.

9

in which we are immoderately involved in hopeless difficulties

by patient accumulation
absolutely inappreciable

and here I become
evident as interest

let us now endure
long isolation

the exploitation of
nothing is easier

impossible to enter here
I believe this simile largely speaks the truth

I cannot doubt
nature's common interest

I cannot but doubt
so many natural and slightly favourable

causes constantly to bear
by some craft, or cycle

a conclusion in whose mind?
as if by some murderous pestilence

I wonder whose turn
will generate which conditions

10

September 27, 2013

that joy
can form

all unreconciled

there might even
be bread

insatiable, ephemeral
and worthy of
intense rides

J

March 26, 2014

despite our disparate roots
prescriptions have been made

operations, extensions
a persistence of

pedalling high, as usual
and perception improbable

Q

October 29, 2013

"*I do not choose to listen*"

scathing timing in the middle
mine's a mid-rational sub-zero
subjection: it's a complicated game
but I am still in

"*hatred, cruelty, ambition, greed, slander*"
(here am I still furious)

there is no matter clear
enough, not even
our outsized selves
in the scathing middle

feel long ahead or
might we coast
readily enough

K

How can we feel much confidence? One remark here is worth a passing notice: we need not marvel – I have given my reasons. Let us now look to our mutual affinities; we cannot hope to explain any "facts," as is so commonly and notoriously the case. But to return to the question of outerwear: if I do not greatly deceive myself, *multiple* values reappear in their intricate weave. Of course this can only be stated in a relative sense, but nothing could be more foolish than to overlook the labour and matter they enfold, or to maintain that a skein of yarn is merely a skein of yarn. Such resemblances will not be revealed (think only of water, for example). Must I explain my meaning more fully?

SPADES

A

(*Lemmium*)

so here I am alone
all along I was
alighting, nor is
this all, I've mistaken
our negative ease
(*for I am never alone*)
for some nebulous tease

2

April 9, 2014

in our mutuality
might we finally
impede our monstrosities

3

March 11, 2014

but in a sideways manner
and shadow-bound
(*unclear*)

louche lineage
logically
(*thus importance
begins*)

undenied, underfunded, like every other
unstretched, untested subject
lurching by

4

frieze no longer
nor focus on
fact's impressions

imprint fragments
fast, in digression's
extremis

dear mantle
whose motley extant sighs
alas, conclusion foregone

5

I'd like a kick
starter camp
pain to get me
out of

bedding base
war-addicted
systems

I have my unknown
technical reasons

6

"such plans are sheer folly"

verses might be
avowed, or
versioned, perhaps they
always vary, saddled with
secret, unsold wants
and vowels

7

♠

February 19, 2014

"going nowhere in particular"

and yet
we bespoke
unconvinced, who could seat
uncease, or assess

8

at least our displeasure has been voiced

9

Senior's last day draws near; let us listen for a moment. We have been involved in the most gratuitous mystery, and can by no means shirk responsibility. Nor can we assign due proportional weight to the following considerations: a thick fossiliferous formation rides here, but to this subject we shall have to return, bearing coats of transformational power (our labour has long been measured in yarn). Let us examine the matter more closely: we have no right to expect fine transitional forms, and once again I can route no satisfactory answer. In addition, I believe in no fixed laws, but this does not now matter. We should not let ourselves be misted by circumstance, or by yarn appearing to have changed its form (and now we grow defiant, for value is mediated through our labour, as has repeatedly been explained). It all shows the absurdity and triviality of such solid views, as if old cotton had never been spun, or berries neither picked nor weighed.

10

November 5, 2013

without work
without speech
without home

but in Nature which never
is more nearly possible
I am now am I now

what a
mean light

men, it is no
light enterprise, nothing
could be as
miserable as

(*can this really*
be said)

war within
a state
which can
no longer

compost the
needs of
others

J

October 26, 2013

the return of breakfast

I have tried to mine
my conduct
are we determined to

(my existence
is *what* kind
of a defect?)

I have tried
to conduct
I could not obtain

ersatz masters and
possessors, visions
even read
a painful seat decline

he's insufferably pretty

there was but one course left
vigorous   extinguished
          proponent

(THE REST WAS NOT PERFECTED)

Q

Sedition

"souls are dyed by thoughts"

plants, nut-hatch, ants, spiders, bees
pirates, parricides, tyrants

blood, bones, the mere fabric of
familiar visits in a strange land

although exhortations were repeated
returns have not been made

wonder seems
seamlessly down-drift

nerves, veins, arteries
do I ever have

(my proximity to impermanence
ineligible here)

an aim in mind
(but from different maps)

exhortation become
a kind of sedition

K

at least we've made known our displeasure

EPILOGUE

On Not Looking into Chapman's Homer

(gleanings for Louis Cabri)

I WENT OUT TO WORK WHEN I WAS NINE

Marrows and parsnips
in the road
a seed grower looping
leaf litter
and, very precious,
a full stomach.

With a little black stick.
I ate them.

Stripping wild and
nothing doing,
only twitching, every little bit
wurzel trim more or less similar.

Some in sacks.
Mother died.
Summer months some of the happiest.

LONG HOURS FOR VERY LITTLE MONEY

Out of puddings, aching limbs.
In the road.
Who did not have symptoms?
Spuds in sacks, who did not
in the shade of
children and girls as well.

A great deal of wheat and barley,
the more hands the better.

All day long sometimes.
The whole steaming
all full of *staying*
away to mind
the baby.

GO BACK TO SINGING AND EATING

Me on a roll.
The hiring comparatively
scarce, hard work invariably
involved. Cockles,
small fish, weeds.

Means test. Invisible
labour also suitable for
women and

Children in the shade of
so rigid that they
were not able.

Too dark to see even
when the weather
is good.

Peel bundle.

Quite ready
for any
meal.

VERY PLEASANT WORK FOR WOMEN

Even the growing of
onions. The sight
did not warp
her nature. Even
the children, expecially.

Rollmops, this excellent
method, I am extremely partial
to this method. Now let us examine
pale skins, soft hands, and
flimsy clothes.

No one can make
such a claim.

Sour does not
mean bad.

A VERY PREGNANT SOCIAL MISCHIEF

Vacuum pump. A supreme
gourmet's delight, girls
at a variety
of jobs few regard
as edible; beer
was consumed.

Posset possessed of
an evil reputation.
They who upload
corn. Salted
turtle eggs, melons,
baskets of pomegranates,
figs, will you
boil that egg?

A vicious aide
indeed.

IT'S SMART TO BE CAREFUL

Blood apricot.
Is she eating?
Well skilled.
Apt to weaken
water texture.
Unweaned, but
tweaked. A fondness
bordering. Usually of
tepid quality, but garnished
so handsomely. The more hands
the better.

Mother and children near
the gate, slight
adjustments may occasionally
be necessary.

EPILOGUE SOURCES

The Epilogue poems are based on texts found in East Vancouver neighbourhood book exchanges.

Benoit, Jehane. *Encyclopedia of Canadian Cooking*. Winnipeg: Greywood Publishing, 1970.

Cottington-Taylor, D.D. *Cadbury's Chocolate Cookery*, 7th ed. Adapted by S. Galloway. Dunedin, New Zealand: Cadbury Fry Hudson, 1962.

Culinary Arts Institute Staff Home Economists. *The Scandinavian Cookbook*. Chicago: Culinary Arts Institute, 1956.

Kitteringham, Jennie. *Country Girls in 19th Century England*. Ruskin College, Oxford: History Workshop Pamphlets, 1973.

Norris, P.E. *About Milk, Cheese, and Eggs*. London: Thorsons Publishers, 1960.

AFTERWORD

In 1776, at the age of sixty-four, an embittered Jean-Jacques Rousseau took to rambling. Feeling rejected, neglected, and condemned, he turned his back on the society in which he had never managed to feel at ease, and found peace wandering the fields outside Paris, noting interesting flora and fauna, and ruminating on his life and career. Rousseau jotted down his philosophical musings on playing cards he carried in his pocket; these notes would form the basis for his final book, *Les rêveries du promeneur solitaire*, translated as *Reveries of the Solitary Walker* (or *a Solitary Walker*). Unfinished at his death and published posthumously in 1782, the *Reveries* reiterate and meditate upon many of Rousseau's central themes: the joys of solitude, the corrupting influence of society, the fragility of happiness and of human relations, and the great, healing solace of nature (not to mention his obsession with enemies and persecution).

Like Rousseau, I too have taken to wandering, though I do so by bicycle. I find cycling particularly conducive to a slow, non-deliberate thinking, an almost sub-conscious contemplation. Biking around Vancouver, my mind often returns to several issues I have long struggled with, my own version of Rousseau's obsessions. I wonder about whether it's really possible or useful to live counter to capitalism's omnipotence in our hyper-capitalist society, about how to live a sustainable life, about how nurturing can truly be valued, and indeed about what value is, and how it gets defined, and to what end. (I also wonder about more mundane things, like what we might make for supper.) What is to be done, I often wonder?

My *Reveries of a Solitary Biker* recycle notes taken from 2013 to 2017 while I was completing a master of arts in Graduate Liberal Studies at Simon Fraser University, and as I biked around the city at that time. During the course of these rides, my mind would wander, sometimes working through particular aspects of whatever I'd been reading, sometimes fixing on more mundane matters. As I rode, I composed by repeating particular lines or phrases over and over under my breath to the rhythm of my riding until they sounded right. Sometimes I would stop to jot down a few pertinent phrases, or what struck me as an interesting combination of words, just enough for me later to reconstruct what I was thinking. I combined these "riding notes" with notes I took while reading, so that my final poems use both my wandering biking thoughts and my readings as source material, just as Rousseau's *Reveries* use his walking meditations as the basis for his ten beautifully constructed "Walks." In homage to the playing-card origins of Rousseau's *Reveries*, my *Reveries* originally were divided into four suits and printed as a deck of cards, in a design by artist Kelly Haydon. The playing-card poems were set to music by my frequent collaborator, clarinetist François Houle; together we can perform the piece by asking audience members to draw some of the cards from the deck; the poems and music are then presented in the order drawn. Each performance is thus distinct, incomplete, and inconclusive.

Although *Reveries of a Solitary Biker* has marked differences from Rousseau's *Reveries*, which I use more as a starting point than as a defining model, the two projects do share common threads. In each of his *Reveries*'s ten walks, Rousseau takes particular moments in his life as catalysts for extended philosophical musings. That is, he extrapolates from the specific and the particular, moving outward from the personal to what he seems to imagine as the universal, or at least the more general. While so doing, he often also seeks to validate his past behaviour, or at least to comprehend it. My *Reveries* share a similar movement outwards from the personal into a wider pondering, although I make no claim to universality. My *Reveries* are also an attempt at least in part to defend my life choices, in particular my decision not to pursue a traditional "career," but instead to spend a good twenty years mainly devoted to raising my children, thinking of myself as a stay-at-home feminist. So that considering the world through the lens of the self, while at the same time trying to decipher how that self is constructed, is something my project inherits from Rousseau.

In addition, Rousseau's *Reveries* are rife with paradox and indeterminacy, like so much of his work, making his method especially suited for adaptation to a consideration of caring labour and my own female experience, sites similarly infused with contradiction and uncertainty. Obviously, my *Reveries*'s card format emphasizes the role of chance, by which Rousseau so often let his life be determined, and which is fundamental to the modernity whose articulation he pioneered. But if as playing cards my *Reveries* highlight contingency, precariousness, and incompletion, as a collaboration they also emphasize love, peaceful contradiction, and a multiplicity of voices, elements vital for the successful negotiation of our current condition. That is, I hope my *Reveries* gesture towards optimistic potential at the same time as they consider seriously our dire reality.

ACKNOWLEDGMENTS

Some of these poems appeared in *The Capilano Review*, *Touch the Donkey*, and *Salvage Journal*; thanks to their editors. Special thanks to my collaborators, Kelly Haydon and François Houle. Thanks also to Steve Collis, Félix Houle, Nina Houle, Steve Duguid, Danielle LaFrance, Jacqueline Leggatt, Carolyn Lesjak, Dorothy Trujillo Lusk for her epigraph from *The Capilano Review* (2015), Molly Rader, Renée Sarojini Saklikar, Sandra Zink, the Simon Fraser University Graduate Liberals Studies program, and my GLS 2013 cohort for their support and encouragement. Thanks to the dedicated folks at Talonbooks. Finally, I must acknowledge and thank the many writers and thinkers whose works have provoked and inspired me. Their words are set inside double quotation marks throughout these poems.

ABOUT THE AUTHOR

Catriona Strang is the author of *Low Fancy* and *Corked*, and co-author with the late Nancy Shaw of *Busted*, *Cold Trip*, and *Light Sweet Crude*. She recently edited *The Gorge: Selected Writing* of Nancy Shaw, and frequently collaborates with composer Jacqueline Leggatt and clarinetist François Houle. A mother of two, she works as editor of *The Capilano Review*.